Walker's American History
series for young people

Where Did You Get Those Eyes?

Where Did You Get Those Eyes?

A Guide to Discovering Your Family History

Kay Cooper

Illustrated by Anthony Accardo

Walker and Company
New York

Walker's American History Series
for Young People

First published in the United States of America in 1988 by the Walker Publishing Company, Inc.

Published simultaneously in Canada by Thomas Allen & Son Canada, Limited, Markham, Ontario.

Library of Congress Cataloging-in-Publication Data

Cooper, Kay.
  Where did you get those eyes? : a guide to discovering your family history / Kay Cooper ; illustrated by Anthony Accardo.
    p.   cm.—(Walker's American history series for young people)
  Bibliography: p.
  Summary: A step-by-step guide for researching one's family tree, from examining inherited traits to interviewing parents and relatives to going through genealogical libraries in search of lost ancestors.
  ISBN 0-8027-6802-4 (trade).   ISBN 0-8027-6803-2 (lib. bdg.)
  1. Genealogy—Juvenile literature.   [1. Genealogy.]   I. Title.
II. Series.
CS15.5.C66 1988
929'.1—dc19
                                                                    88-149
                                                                      CIP
                                                                      AC

Printed in the United States of America

10 9 8 7 6 5 4 3 2 1

Book design by Laurie McBarnette

This book is dedicated to families—all of them every-where—particularly to my brother, Charles Stevens Cooper, who is the last male descendant in our Cooper family line.

Acknowledgements

The author acknowledges the kind assistance of the following people: Anna Vasconcelles, archivist, Illinois State Archives; Mary Reynolds, head librarian, Champaign Illinois State Branch Genealogical Library of the Church of Jesus Christ of Latter-day Saints; Georgie B. Cooper, teacher, Brea Junior High School, Brea, California; William A. Sausaman, genealogist, Springfield, Illinois; Naaman J. Woodland Jr., Department of History, LaMar University, Beaumont, Texas.

Special thanks to Leona M. Brown, Flint, Michigan; Katherine Pauley, teacher, Springfield (Illinois) School District 186; Kathryn Ransom, reading coordinator, Springfield Public Schools; David C. DeBoe, director of educational services, The Texas State Historical Association, Austin, Texas; Marilyn Ames, teacher, Sibley, Illinois; Mrs. Lyle Linenweber, Bloomington, Illinois; Terry Johnson-Cooney, Chicago, Illinois; and Stuart Anderson, Courtney Wind, Josh Jacobson, and Kim McDevitt of Springfield, Illinois.

Contents

Looking into Family Faces

Has anyone ever told you that your eyes are the same color as one of your parents' eyes? Or that your smile is like that of a relative you've never met? Or that you don't look like anyone else in your family?

Cordelia Hanks Angell of Bloomington, Illinois, has on her right cheek a mole—a trait that has been passed down through her family. Her grandfather's second cousin, President Abraham Lincoln, had a mole on his right cheek, too. Mrs. Angell also has high cheek bones, as Lincoln did. Looking into her face, you can see hints of Lincoln's face. There is a family likeness between Mrs. Angell and the president. That likeness was passed down through Mrs. Angell's great-grandfather, Joshua Hanks, who was a first cousin to Nancy Hanks, Abraham Lincoln's mother.

Almost an exact likeness in appearance, height, and in-

High cheek bones and a mole on the right cheek were passed down to this woman, Cordelia Hanks Angell, and to President Abraham Lincoln from their ancestors.

Courtesy of the Illinois State Historical Library Illinois History

telligence was passed from the president down to his only grandson, Abraham Lincoln II. Many people thought that young Lincoln would become a second President Lincoln when he grew up, but he died at age sixteen in England.

Do you know whom you most resemble in your family? Find some pictures of your parents and grandparents when they were your age. Compare their faces with yours. Whom do you most resemble? Family faces help tell you who you are. Your physical features, and even parts of your personality, have been passed down to you from your ancestors. You might say that looking at yourself in the mirror is like looking into the faces of your ancestors. Each of your ancestors has given you something to make you the special person that you are. Even if you don't have the same color of eyes as anyone else in your immediate family, you can be sure one of your ancestors had your eye color.

Discovering who this person was can be very exciting. You may even find that your eye color isn't the only thing you have in common. In a search for her ancestors, a high-school student in Austin, Texas, discovered that she was very much like a grandmother she had never met. She found that she was taking courses in high school similar to those her grandmother had taken, and that they were interested in the same subjects.

Who you are—from your appearance down to your interests, talents, habits, and values—depends a lot on your parents, grandparents, and great-grandparents. If you have a special talent or ability, such as a good singing voice or the ability to work hard math problems, that talent or ability was passed down to you from your ancestors.

The famous German musician Johann Sebastian Bach, for example, had a grandfather and great-grandfather who were musicians. Bach had twenty children, all of whom had musical talent. Three became well known for their music.

The desire and ability to be a leader of government seems to be passed down through families. Several U.S. presidents, for example, were related. John Adams, the second president, was the father of John Quincy Adams, the sixth president. Richard Nixon's distant cousins are William H. Taft and Herbert Hoover. James Madison was a second cousin of Zachary Taylor. Theodore Roosevelt and Franklin Delano Roosevelt were fifth cousins. Ulysses S. Grant was a fourth cousin of Franklin D. Roosevelt and a distant cousin of Grover Cleveland. And George Washington and Queen Elizabeth I of England were cousins.

As you uncover your family history, you may discover that you are related to a famous person. You might be proud to find out that you're related to this person. It is just as exciting, however, to find out why your ancestor settled along the New England coast and what he did for a living. Who knows what you'll discover about yourself and your family. Remember, even a dishonest ancestor has a story to tell.

Investigating your family history is a process called genealogy. The word *genealogy* comes from two Greek words: *genea*, meaning "family," and the suffix *-logy* meaning "study." Genealogy not only tells your family history, it tells you who you are.

By uncovering your family history, you might discover why your ancestors came to America. Where they came from. When. And why they came.

When GiGi Neill was a high-school student in McCamey, Texas, she uncovered her family history. She traced her father's family back 250 years to William Neill. Neill came to Pennsylvania from Ireland in 1730. GiGi was excited to discover that her family took part in the development of the United States. Her ancestors were farmers who cleared the land, soldiers who fought in the American Revolution and the Civil War, and adventurers who joined the California Gold Rush in hopes of finding wealth.

Your family might be part of American history, and part of the history of other countries. As you explore your ancestors' lives, you will get to know them as real people. Their experiences will become yours, as if *you* are the settler, for example, who walked the Indian trails from Virginia to Kentucky, or the soldier who took up arms to fight in the Civil War. Your ancestors are your special link to the past.

So, get ready for a lot of surprises as you begin your search for your family's faces from earlier times. It's a search that will take you to new places and put you in touch with interesting people. You may even find a forgotten cemetery, locate a lost relative, or explore places where your ancestors once lived.

The Search Begins with You

Your search begins when you first wonder who helped make you the special person you are. In genealogy, you start with a history about yourself and your immediate family and then work toward completing a history about your grandparents and great-grandparents.

First, find out all the information you can about yourself. What is your full name? When is your birthday? When did you have your first haircut and lose your first tooth? What costumes have you worn for Halloween? Who has been your best friend for the longest time?

You can put together a good history from what you remember about your life so far. You can also ask your parents, older brothers and sisters, and other family members about yourself. And you can learn from documents. Your birth certificate, baby book, report cards, award certificates, diaries, old letters, and family pictures, for example, will tell you about your own history.

Your parents can help you find documents for your history. These documents will help you piece together important events in your life. Some may help you remember events which you've forgotten.

Ask relatives and family friends what they remember about your life. Do they remember anything about your first day at school? Or your first birthday party, or who your best friend was in kindergarten? Maybe they noticed you were especially good at drawing or with building blocks when you were young.

Making Your Own Time Line

Once you've collected all the information you can find about yourself, you can make a chart of your life with a "time line" that shows the events most important to you.

You'll need some 8½-by-11-inch or 9-by-12-inch white paper, one sheet for every year of your life. Tape the sheets together to make one long piece. Then draw a straight line lengthwise across the middle of each sheet of paper. This line is your "time line." Give each sheet a number for each year of your life. Begin with your birth date at the left end of the line, and end with the sheet marked with your age today. Next to your age, sign your name and write today's date.

Fill in the people and events that are important to you above and below the time line. You might include the name of your favorite teacher, the names of pets, family vacations, school events, and favorite songs or TV shows. For example, above or below the line on sheet 1 you might write "My first birthday," and make a list of the people who came to see you that day.

Or, you might want to record your feelings on your time

line. Fill in the events that made you feel happy, sad, proud, scared, weak, strong, or grown-up. Next to each event, write how you felt. For example, events that made you feel grown-up might have been your first crush on a movie star or your decision to play for a baseball team. Perhaps a divorce or death in your family made you feel sad.

You also can use your time line to mark changes in your life. These changes might include how your personal appearance changed, how you improved a particular skill, or when you moved from one house or apartment to another. You can illustrate these changes in words or drawings.

For fun, try adding more paper to the end of your time line and make an imaginary, future time line. Imagine that you are seventy-five years old. What do you want your children and grandchildren to know about you? How do you want to be remembered? Write down your ideas. Draw a picture of yourself at age seventy-five.

Preserving Your Time Line

Get permission to put your time line on your bedroom wall. Add paper and more information to it as you grow older. See if you can get your brother or sister or a friend to make their own time lines, and then compare your time line with theirs. You'll discover ways that other people are like, or not like, you.

Whatever you do, don't throw your time line away. Keep it safe by putting it in a cardboard mailing tube, which you can buy at a stationery store. A closet shelf or dresser drawer is a good place to store the tube.

By making a time line about yourself, you've started putting together your own history. In later years, perhaps you can help your children make their time lines, and compare your time line with theirs. You will discover how much your children are like, or not like, you. And they will learn what life was like for you when you were their age.

What Else Happened on Your Birthday?

Ask your parents, other family members, and neighbors to think of events that happened on the day you were born. What went on that day? Talk to your grandparents or an older brother or sister. What do they remember about the day? Are there funny stories about the day you were born? Does anyone remember a national or local news story from that day?

Compare what you learn from family and friends with a newspaper account of the day. Your public library may have past issues of newspapers on microfilm—a type of film used to photograph documents and make them much smaller. If so, ask the librarian if the library has a newspaper from the day you were born. You can have any page of the newspaper copied from the microfilm for about 25 cents a page. You also may want a copy of the page that carries your birth announcement. Since some newspapers don't print birth announcements every day, you may have to check several newspaper issues to find the announcement of your birth.

What else happened on your birthday? You'll be surprised at how many important events took place the day you were born. Go to the reference section of the library. Reference books cannot be checked out, but you can use them to take notes. The reference books that follow will help you discover other years when your birth date was important.

BOOKS THAT WILL HELP YOU DISCOVER WHAT ELSE HAPPENED ON YOUR BIRTHDAY

THIS BOOK:

DOES THE FOLLOWING:

The Book of Days, Vols. 1 and 2, by Robert Chambers. Published by Gale Research Company, Book Tower, Detroit, Michigan, 1967.

Lists historical events over the centuries.

The American Book of Days, Third Edition, compiled and edited by Jane M. Hatch. Published by The H. W. Wilson Company, New York, 1978.

Gives holidays and historical events in the United States for every day of the year.

Finding Records at Home

Now that you've discovered information about yourself and recorded it on a time line, you are ready to discover information about your parents, grandparents, and great-grandparents. Keeping track of all the facts you'll be finding will be easier if you use an ancestor chart. This chart shows you as a child of your parents, and puts you on a line between your father and mother. If you are adopted, you can use this same chart to do a history of your adopted family.

You are listed as number 1—the first generation—on your chart. A generation is the average time between the births of your parents and their children, or about twenty-five to thirty years.

Use a ruler to help you draw a chart like the one on page 15. Write your full name in ink on the line next to the number 1. If you have a nickname, write it in parentheses beside your given name. Write your birthday next to "b." First write the day, then the month's abbreviation, then the year. Next to "p.b." write where you were born in the following order: town, county, and state. Above your name, write the color of your eyes, or use a crayon to show the color.

Your father is number 2. Write in ink your father's full name. A father's number is always double the number in front of his child's name. Your father's father—your grandfather—has a number double that of your father. So, your father's father's number is 4.

Your mother is number 3. A mother's number is always double her child's, plus one. Use ink to write your mother's full name, using the name she was given at birth and her last name at that time.

As you can see, you've now divided your chart. The top half of the page will be your father's side of the family. The bottom half will be your mother's side.

The numbers continue for each generation, always starting with the male on your father's side. So, all the even numbers are men. All the uneven numbers are women.

Ask your parents for their birth dates (b.) and where they were born (p.b.). Then write down when (m.) and where (p.m.) they were married. If your parents are deceased, write down when (d.) and where (p.d.) they died. Add the color of their eyes. Now you've completed your parents', or the second, generation.

Your ancestor chart begins to branch like a tree at your grandparents', or third, generation. Ancestor charts are sometimes called "family trees" because each new branch forms another family group. As your tree grows, however, filling in the names and dates of the next generation becomes harder. Ask your parents to help you. (*See* "Questions To Ask Your Parents" on page 16.) Write in the day,

Family Tree

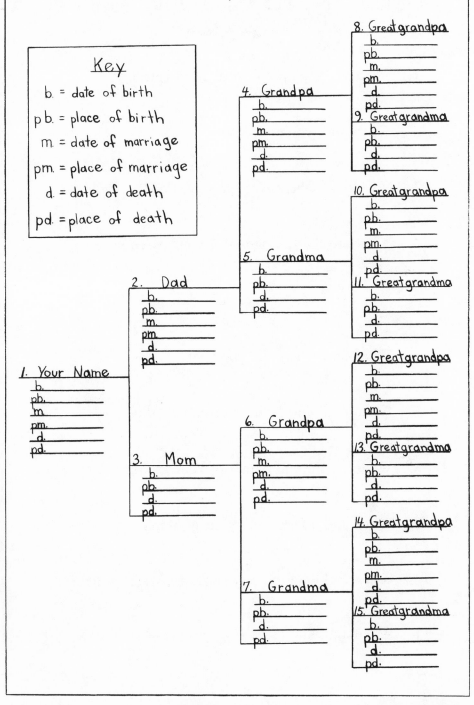

Key

b. = date of birth

p b. = place of birth

m. = date of marriage

pm. = place of marriage

d. = date of death

pd. = place of death

1. Your Name
b.
pb.
m.
pm.
d.
pd.

2. Dad
b.
pb.
m.
pm.
d.
pd.

3. Mom
b.
pb.
d.
pd.

4. Grandpa
b.
pb.
m.
pm.
d.
pd.

5. Grandma
b.
pb.
d.
pd.

6. Grandpa
b.
pb.
m.
pm.
d.
pd.

7. Grandma
b.
pb.
d.
pd.

8. Greatgrandpa
b.
pb.
m.
pm.
d.
pd.

9. Greatgrandma
b.
pb.
d.
pd.

10. Greatgrandpa
b.
pb.
m.
pm.
d.
pd.

11. Greatgrandma
b.
pb.
d.
pd.

12. Greatgrandpa
b.
pb.
m.
pm.
d.
pd.

13. Greatgrandma
b.
pb.
d.
pd.

14. Greatgrandpa
b.
pb.
m.
pm.
d.
pd.

15. Greatgrandma
b.
pb.
d.
pd.

QUESTIONS TO ASK YOUR PARENTS

1. What is the name on your birth certificate?

2. When and where were you born?

3. When and where were you married?

4. What are the full names of your parents?

5. When and where were your parents born?

6. When and where did your parents marry?

7. When and where did your parents die?

8. What are the full names of your grandparents?

9. When and where were your grandparents born?

10. When and where did your grandparents marry?

11. When and where did your grandparents die?

month, and year for all the dates. Always write the complete year, not just the last two numbers.

Since full names, dates, and places may be wrong, use a pencil to write down your grandparents' information. When you know the information is correct, go over it with a pen. This way, you can see what is known—written in ink—and what is not known—written in pencil—on your chart.

For example, maybe your mother thinks her father was born in Kansas because he said he grew up there. But perhaps he was born somewhere else, and then moved to Kansas. You would write "Kansas" in pencil and change it to ink when you found better proof that he really was born in Kansas.

Now you need to find out about your eight great-grandparents. How can you do this? You probably will be looking at many blank spaces and words written in pencil as you try to complete your chart. How do you find people and information that have been missing seventy-five to one hundred years?

Getting Organized

Before you begin looking for missing ancestors, dates, and places, set up a history/mystery notebook. A history/mystery notebook contains your family's history and unsolved mysteries—missing information that is needed to complete your ancestor chart.

For your notebook, you need a three-ring binder, a hole punch, three-hole notepaper, and eight dividers. Insert your ancestor chart at the front of your notebook. The hole punch is useful when you put in this page. Next, write your last name, also called your surname, on a divider and place it after your chart. Your mother's maiden name—her last name at birth—goes on the next divider. Then use a divider for each of the other six surnames on your ancestor chart.

Now, about those unsolved mysteries. Who told you where grandpa was born? Your mother, right?

Arm yourself with your notebook and a pencil. Ask your mother again about grandpa's birthplace, or about any other unsolved mysteries. Why does she think he was born in Kansas? Who told her? Who might know for sure? What documents would prove where he was born? Where are these documents?

In your notebook, write down as much information as you can get from each interview. For example, when you ask your mother about her side of the family, write your mother's maiden name and the date of the interview at the top of the page. Then, on the upper right-hand corner of the page, write the name of the person you are trying to find out about. It's helpful if you also add the "code number"—the number before every person's full name on your ancestor chart. Your mother's father's number, for example, is 6. Include a person's code number on any page that you add to your notebook.

Place the pages about your ancestors after the dividers on which you've written their surnames. This makes your record-keeping easier because you have everything about your ancestors with the same surname together in one place. Later, when you find a birth place or date written in a family Bible or on a marriage record, you can copy this information and add it to your notebook. Be sure to write down the source for each piece of information you find. If you note the source and then come across two or more different birth dates for the same person, you'll be able to decide which source is likely to give you the best information.

When you search for missing information, look for original sources—the first recordings of names, dates and events.

Original sources include marriage licenses, birth and death certificates, newspaper articles, and letters. Original sources usually give you more accurate information than secondary sources, such as copied records. These are written by people who have studied the original sources. They may have made a mistake when they copied the original sources.

Looking for Original Sources

Original sources may be easier to find than you think. Look around you—they may have been put away and forgotten. Ask your parents if you can go digging through trunks or boxes in the attic, cellar, or storage closets.

You are looking for birth and death certificates, marriage licenses, school records, address books, Bibles, wills, newspaper clippings, old letters, and diaries. And don't overlook postcards, insurance papers, passports, old family albums, pictures, and quilts with names on them. Check the backs of photographs, the front pages of old books, and names in guest books from funerals and other functions. One of these items may prove where an ancestor was born or died. Or you might find a sentence about an ancestor's marriage written on a page of an old letter or diary.

Once you find these items, get permission to organize them in a safe place. Set up a file of 3-by-5-inch index cards. Make out one card for each item you find. On each card, print the name of the item, where it is kept, and what information it contains. Some objects, such as letters and birth certificates, should be put in large folders or manila envelopes. Pictures should be stored in a metal box and kept in a dry place where dampness and dirt can't reach them.

The information on these original sources may help you complete your ancestor chart. Record the information about each ancestor on a page in your notebook and place it after the divider with the same surname. Remember to include the person's code number on the page. If you have information on the page which you can add to your ancestor chart, write it in the correct place on your chart.

Hidden Stories in Pictures

Old family pictures may provide clues to names, dates, and places, if the pictures are labeled. If they are not labeled, you can compare the pictures with others that appear to come from the same time period. Try to find a family member who can tell you who the unknown people are. If you have many pictures that are mysterious, choose a few that interest you the most. Here are some tips to help you discover who the people are in the picture, when the picture was taken, and where it was taken.

To help you date your pictures, look at the subjects of the photographs. Notice the clothing and hair styles worn by the people, for example. Compare the styles with pictures in books, or ask someone who knows a lot about fashion to help you guess the time period. Other subjects that may be helpful to you include cars, household appliances, and the appearance of familiar landmarks, such as buildings and bridges. All of these can give clues about the date the picture was taken.

Look closely at the clothes and jewelry worn. You can use a magnifying glass to help you see details better. Someone in your family still may have the clothes in the picture, or a ring, pin, or necklace. Jewelry may be inscribed with dates and initials. An old trunk in your grandparent's attic may contain the very dress you see in a photo!

What objects are in the photos? Maybe the person in your photo is holding something, or perhaps an object lies on a nearby chair or table. Objects are good clues. People

This photo was dated by a family member who remembers that the Saint Bernard dog was a family pet and lived in the late 1930s. Another clue to the date is the car in the background. It is a 1935 Master Chevrolet, the only model with "suicide" doors. A suicide door has a handle at the front of the door instead of the back. The door, which opens in front, is dangerous because the wind can catch it and pull it open.

Courtesy of K. Ransom

usually have themselves photographed with things that are important to them. Perhaps a family member remembers when a particular object was purchased.

How are your ancestors posed in the photos? Are they standing or seated? Do you see a person's complete face or only one side of it? Photography was invented in the early 1800s, but film wasn't invented until the 1880s. Before the 1880s, photographers used wet or dry plates made of metal or glass on which to take pictures. These plates had to be exposed to light for a long time so that images could form on the plates. Long exposures made poses difficult to hold, so people often posed with their elbows resting on the back of a chair or a hand resting on a railing. People in these photos, therefore, look very formal and seldom smile.

Copying Photographs

It may be a good idea to make copies of old photographs so that you can mail them to relatives who might help you name the people.

Use a photocopying machine, making sure you push the "extra dark" button so that the picture can be easily seen. Send a letter explaining that you are working on your family history and that you want to know who the unknown people are. If possible, you'd also like to know when the picture was taken, and where.

Family Group Sheets

As you look for information about your ancestors, you'll probably come across a record that lists several people with the same surname. These people may or may not be from the same family. For example, look in your telephone book and see how many people have the same surname as one of the families on your ancestor chart. Maybe someone listed in your phone book even has the same first name, as well as the same surname, as one of your ancestors.

How will you be able to pick out your ancestor from all the people who have his or her name? One way is to know the names of your ancestor's brothers and sisters. Your grandfather, for example, might be listed on the record with his siblings. You'll know this person is your grandfather because he is listed with his brothers and sisters. Even if he is an only child, he can be identified because he'll be listed without brothers and sisters.

There is another reason why knowing the names of brothers and sisters is useful. You might discover that you cannot find any information about a particular ancestor on your chart. When this happens, try to find information about that ancestor's brothers or sisters. You might be surprised to discover that a brother or sister left a family history with all the information you need about your ancestor.

The form which follows, called a family group sheet, will help you keep track of all the brothers and sisters of the people on your ancestor chart. You can make these sheets yourself, or you can order them from Netti Schreiner-Yantis, 6818 Lois Drive, Springfield, Virginia 22150. Keep your family group sheets in your notebook and file each sheet after the proper surname.

Start with one sheet for each married couple on your ancestor chart. That's seven sheets—one for your parents, and one for each set of grandparents and great-grandparents.

For your own family, write your father's full name and his number (2) on the line after "Family of." Then fill in the information about your father, mother, yourself, and each brother and sister in the proper places on the sheet.

The circles on the sheet are for your sources. List your-

FAMILY GROUP SHEET

Husband's Code . . . .
Wife's Code . . . .

FATHER'S NAME _____

Date of Birth _____ Place _____

Date of Death _____ Place _____

Present Address (or) Place of Burial _____

His Father _____ His Mother's Maiden Name _____

Date of Marriage of HUSBAND and WIFE on this sheet _____ Place _____

Check here if there was another marriage: By husband ☐ By Wife ☐   Was this couple divorced? Yes ☐ No ☐   When? _____

MOTHER'S MAIDEN NAME _____ (Use separate sheet for each marriage)

Date of Birth _____ Place _____

Date of Death _____ Place _____

Present Address (or) Place of Burial _____

Her Father _____ Her Mother's Maiden Name _____

Items of interest about the above couple (occupations, hobbies, achievements; social, civil, and political activities; physical descriptions—include photos if possible; military service; cause of death):

Use reverse side for additional information

Have family sheet		CHILDREN (Arrange in order of birth)	Code	Birth Information	Death Information	Marriage Information
	1			ON _____ AT	ON _____ AT	ON _____ TO
	2			ON _____ AT	ON _____ AT	ON _____ TO
	3			ON _____ AT	ON _____ AT	ON _____ TO
	4			ON _____ AT	ON _____ AT	ON _____ TO
	5			ON _____ AT	ON _____ AT	ON _____ TO

Check here if there are additional children ☐

Footnoting. To substantiate the information recorded on this page, please use the footnotes listed below. One of these numbers should be placed in the circle provided next to each answer on the questionnaire. If you got the information from a source not listed, place that source on a vacant line and use the number next to which it has been placed as your footnote number.

Use ① only if you have filled in the blank from personal knowledge (such as the name of your brother). If you must look up his marriage date, give as the source wherever you looked it up. If you asked him, give his name as the source.

① **Name and address of person filling in this sheet.** Date _____

② _____

③ _____

④ _____

⑤ _____

⑥ _____

⑦ _____

⑧ _____

self as the number 1 source. This means that you have personal knowledge of a fact. You know, for example, your full name. Write your full name in the proper place and write number 1 in the circle. Your number 3 source might be "my mother told me." Perhaps she told you the date of your birth. Write this date in the proper place and write the number 3 in the circle.

It's important to record the sources of information on your family group sheet. Your sources will help you solve a problem when you find conflicting facts. For example, your dad may tell you his father's full name. But then you find that your grandpa's first name on his birth certificate is different. If you have this problem, write each full name in the proper column and draw a second circle after the second name. Enter the appropriate numbers for your sources in the circles. Because the birth certificate is the source nearest in time and place to the day your grandpa was named, it is the more correct one. So enter the name from his birth certificate from your family group sheet to your ancestor chart.

Now that you have an idea about the kind of forms you'll be filling out for your family history, you are ready to go on to the following chapters.

Dear Grandma,   Nov. 5, 1987

I am working
our family tree
I need your help
filled in as
information as
the ancestor chart
many
can

Interviewing
Relatives

One of the best ways to solve mysteries on your ancestor chart, such as the color of great-grandpa's eyes or the birth date of great-grandma, is to interview the oldest member on each side of your family. If this person lives close to you, arm yourself with your history/mystery notebook, pencils, and a note pad on which to take notes. Show your relative your ancestor chart and your family group sheets, especially the blank sections and the sections written in pencil. Does your relative remember the color of great-grandpa's eyes, or great-grandma's birth date?

If your relative can't remember exact dates, other dates, such as historical dates, might help both of you. For example, was great-grandma born before World War I (1914–1921)? Did she die before the Korean War (1950–1953)?

Show your relative the family photos you've had trouble identifying. Does your relative know some of the people

An interview with the oldest living member of this family might help find the names of all these brothers and sisters. The clothing and hair styles can help date the photo.
Courtesy of William A. Sausaman

in the pictures? When and where was each of them born? Are any of them still living? If so, can you get their addresses so that you can interview or write them?

While you're interviewing, don't try to write down every word your relative says. Instead, write down key words and phrases, and use abbreviations. For example, you might write, "Grandpa. br. eyes. teased others. related to Daniel Boone? record in Reading, Pa, newspaper or old prayer book. Aunt Liz has it?"

If your relative gets off the subject, ask questions that lead him or her back to the topic, such as "That's interesting that grandpa liked baseball. Did his father like baseball, too? What was grandpa's father's full name?"

If your relative replies only "yes" or "no" to your questions, ask him or her to go into greater detail. You might ask, for example, "Was he tall, average height, or short? What physical features do you remember? Did he have a beard or mustache? How did she wear her hair? What were his or her special talents and abilities?"

If an answer is unclear, don't be afraid to ask your relative to explain the answer to you. You might not know the location of a birthplace or know which child your relative is talking about.

Family interviews are also good opportunities to locate any documents that might help verify the names and dates on your chart. For example, try to find a family Bible that has been passed down for several generations. Ask if someone in the family has kept newspaper clippings of family events or a quilt with embroidered signatures of ancestors on it. You might get this person's address so that you can find out more about the clippings or quilt.

When you return home from your interview, go over your notes to make sure you understand what your relative said. If you are unsure about some of your notes, call your relative on the telephone to check your facts. You may need to visit your relative again and fill in more information.

After each interview, put your notes in your notebook. Make sure you put your notes in the proper place for each ancestor. Remember to head each page with the source of information and to use the code number. Then record the information on your family group sheets and enter it on your ancestor chart.

Checking the Accuracy of Family Mystery Stories

Many families have stories that have been passed down from generation to generation by word of mouth. Often these stories become exaggerated with the imagination of the teller. Perhaps in your family someone claims to be related to a famous person or to someone who invented a machine.

In some cases, these family mystery stories cannot be proven. But you can check out the facts to see if the stories are correct.

For example, suppose you are trying to find out if your grandpa was related to a famous person. Interview two or more relatives on the topic. Check whether they agree with one another and also check the available sources of information that might prove or disprove the story. If one source is accurate, it's probably safe for you to conclude that your grandpa was related to this famous person. So, *you* have a famous relative!

Is it possible you have an inventor in the family? Ask several relatives the following questions:

- What was the inventor's full name?
- During what time period was the machine invented?
- What did the machine do?
- How did the machine work?

- Was the inventor working with another person or for a company or industry when he invented the machine? What was the name of this person, company, or industry?
- What was the name of the company or industry that used the machine?

The more answers you have to the above questions, the more likely you are to solve your family's inventor story.

Call your local public library and ask where the nearest collection of the annual indexes to the U.S. patents are located. They may be in your local public library, or in a state, historical, or university library. Go there and ask the librarian to help you locate the patent for the machine you're interested in. The patent, which is an original source, will tell you who is credited for the invention.

Make a Tape

One of the best ways to preserve family history is to interview your relatives on tape. Focus your interview on specific people, such as your grandmother's parents, brothers, and sisters. Or, interview your immediate family and ask questions about yourself to record facts about the day you were born. To clear up family mystery stories, interview more than one relative about the mystery. Listen to the interviews, then talk to each person again to clear up any conflicting facts.

Before the interview, practice using the tape recorder to make sure it works properly. Bring at least two tapes and extra batteries to the interview.

At the beginning of the tape, identify the person you're interviewing, the date, and the location of the interview.

When you're back home, label the tape with the full name of the person you've interviewed and the date of the interview. Store the tape in a safe place. If the tape contains

FACT-FINDING SHEET

FAMILY OF _____

ADDRESS _____

	Husband	**Wife**
Full Name		
Date of Birth		
Place of Birth		
Date of Marriage		
Place of Marriage		
Date of Death		
Place of Death		
Place of Burial		
Does Grave Have Monument?		
Full Name of Mother (including maiden name)		
Full Name of Father		

Note: Please fill in vertical columns for both husband and wife, including names of parents of each.

	First Child	Second Child	Third Child	Fourth Child
Full Name				
Date of Birth				
Place of Birth				
Date of Death				
Place of Death				
Place of Burial				

information that you need to fill in your family group sheets and ancestor chart, record it in your history/mystery notebook. Make sure you also record the information about the interview in the proper place in your notebook. Head the page with the source of information and use the code number. Write down the place where you stored the tape.

Writing Relatives for Information

A copy of your ancestor chart and a questionnaire, like the fact-finding sheet on page 32, can be sent to relatives who live far away. You might write:

Dear _____,

I'm working on our family tree and I need your help. I've filled in as much information as I can on the ancestor chart and the fact-finding sheet, but there are still some blanks. Whatever you can fill in on the fact-finding sheet would be helpful. I've enclosed a self-addressed, stamped envelope so you can return it to me. I'll send you a copy of our family tree when it is complete. Thanks so much for your help!

Love, _____

Be sure to enclose a copy of your ancestor chart, a copy of the fact-finding sheet, and a self-addressed, stamped envelope with your letter.

Places to Continue Your Search

Now that you have found all the information you can find at home, and have visited or written your relatives, take another look at your ancestor chart. You may still have mysteries to solve. How can you continue to research your genealogy?

It's a good idea to focus your research on either your father's or your mother's side of the family. Choose one ancestor whom you want to know more about. For this person, you should know

1. The person's name
2. The approximate dates he or she lived
3. The places he or she lived

With this information, you can begin to search outside your home and family for facts.

First, set a simple goal. Try to find *one* item of information—a name, date, place—that is needed to complete your ancestor chart. Perhaps you need to find the middle or maiden name of a person, or the exact date or place of a person's birth, marriage, or death.

The information you need might be in records involving your ancestor. These records—a birth certificate, marriage license, and death certificate, for example—were made during your ancestor's life or immediately after death. Look for them first in areas where your ancestors lived. You might find these records by visiting one of the following places.

Public Library

The public library in your town or city is probably the best place to search for information. It may have a genealogy collection—books, newspaper clippings, and records about people who lived in your particular area during a certain time period. If your ancestor lived in the area during this time period, you may find exactly what you need. If you need a newspaper from another city, or a census record that is not part of the public library's collection, the librarian can borrow it for you from libraries throughout the United States, or from state and national archives. A section in this chapter tells you more about census records.

You also can write the public library closest to the place where your ancestor lived and ask the librarian there for information about your ancestor. You can find the address of the library you need by going to the reference section in your public library. Ask the librarian for the *American Library Directory*. These two volumes, published and compiled by The R. R. Bowker Company of New York City, list libraries by state and then by city. Find the address you need and write the librarian.

You might write "I am working on my family history

and need to know when my great-grandmother, Elizabeth Davidson Edwards, died. I know she died in Calhoun County, probably in 1912 or 1913. Do you have any information you could send me on her exact date of death?"

Be sure to enclose a stamped envelope addressed to yourself with your letter.

Asking the Librarian for Help

Keep in mind that the librarian can be one of your best resources for information. Tell the librarian that you're working on your family history, and make it plain what you want to know. Ask specific questions, such as "My great-grandmother was born before 1900, but I don't know her birth date. Where can I find it?"

Often librarians have interesting ideas on how to go about finding information on ancestors. So, ask for help!

Census Records

The best sources to use in the library are the federal and state census records. A census is a count of the population in a state (state census) or in the entire United States (federal census). A federal census is taken for the purpose of determining how many representatives in the United States Congress each state is entitled to have. A census has been taken every ten years since 1790.

State censuses are taken during the years between federal censuses to determine how many representatives in state legislatures each state voting district is entitled to have. Sometimes state censuses are taken for special purposes, such as counting all the people in the state who served in a particular war.

If your mystery ancestor lived during the period 1850 to 1900, census records are the first records you should seek for information. The census records are available at the National Archives in Washington, D.C., which is the nation's official place to store records made by the federal government. All have been microfilmed, and your public library may have microfilm copies of these records. If it does not, the librarian can rent them for you.

If your ancestor lived during the year 1900 in the United States, start with the 1900 federal census because this record gives the best information on families. Your ancestor's full name, date and place of birth, dates and places of birth of all his or her children, and occupation are some of the facts you'll uncover in this record. You'll also discover if your ancestor could read, write, and speak English.

Ask the librarian to help you locate the census record in which you're interested. Since many censuses are indexed by county and then by township (if the township was formed), you'll need to *know the county* in which your ancestor lived in the year the census was taken. Your search will be easier if you also know the township.

If your ancestor lived in the United States during the period from 1910 to now, you cannot use the federal census records to find information about your ancestor. The government considers these records "confidential" and won't release them. You can, however, request a copy of a specific record for these years from the Bureau of the Census Office, U. S. Department of Commerce, Pittsburg, Kansas 66762. If you need a record of a living ancestor, you must ask this person to obtain the record for you. If you need a record of a deceased ancestor, you must send the bureau a copy of the person's death certificate.

Be sure to ask the librarian if any state censuses were made during your ancestor's lifetime. If these records exist, ask the librarian if they are available for your use.

Writing State and Federal Agencies

The Directory in the back of this book lists several places you can write for information.

If you write a state or federal agency, ask the agency to send you the correct form for ordering the record, and ask the price. Always enclose a stamped envelope addressed to yourself for a reply.

Branch Genealogical Libraries of the Mormon Church

Chances are good that you can find information about your mystery ancestor in the genealogical records of the Mormon Church. This church has the largest collection of genealogical materials in the world at Salt Lake City, Utah. You don't have to be a member of the Church of Jesus Christ of Latter-day Saints to use this library or one of its branches. And your ancestors didn't have to be Mormons to have records about them included in the Mormon collection.

Through the church's branch libraries, you can get copies of records from the collection in Salt Lake City. You must use these records in the branch library, however. Branch librarians usually do not answer questions through the mail.

The records in the Salt Lake City collection date back several hundred years and come from over 40 countries, including the United States, England, Scotland, Ireland, Germany, Mexico, and countries in Central and South America. Records on Africa include basic history, maps, and books which will tell you what genealogical materials can be found in major African libraries. The church also has records on American Indians. These records are indexed by tribe. Presently, church members are filming records in China and Hungary to add to their vast collection. So if your ancestor lived in one of these countries, you soon may be able to obtain a copy of a record with his or her name on it.

Through the branch library, you also can get copies of most county records of the United States up to about 1850 to 1900. County records include birth certificates, marriage licenses, wills, and death records. If you need the exact date or place of an ancestor's birth, marriage, or death, ask the librarian to help you locate the county record that may give you this information.

To find the branch library nearest you, look in the Yellow Pages of your local and area telephone books under the heading "Churches." Then look under "Church—Latter-day Saints." Call the church office and ask for the address, telephone number, and library hours of the genealogical branch library nearest you. There are over 460 branches in the world.

If there isn't a Mormon church in your area, then write to this address: Branch Genealogical Libraries, The Genealogical Society, 50 East North Temple St., Salt Lake City, Utah 84150. Ask for the name and address of the branch library nearest your residence, the telephone number, and the library hours.

Cemeteries

A walk through a cemetery can be a journey through your family history. Until the mid-1900s, many family members lived together in the same area of the United States and were buried in the same cemetery. If you know of a cemetery where some of your ancestors are buried, but can't visit it, write the cemetery office and ask for information about the ancestor in whom you are interested. Give the person's name and the date of death, if possible. Remember to enclose a stamped envelope addressed to yourself for reply.

If you're close enough to visit the cemetery, arm yourself with a notebook, pencils, white chalk, and a camera, and go there. It's a good idea to call the cemetery office before you visit to find out the days and hours the office is open.

When you arrive at the cemetery, visit the office. Tell the person there that you are working on your family history. Ask the person to help you find the location of your ancestor's grave.

Once you find the grave, copy the inscription on the tombstone letter for letter. Include all punctuation marks and enclose what you think is missing in parentheses.

(E)liza, Wife of
Char(les) Log(an)

Sometimes old inscriptions are hard to read. You may find it helpful to shade the inscription with your hand so the sun doesn't cast shadows over the writing. Or you can use your white chalk to trace over the writing and make it easier to read.

The inscription usually gives the name, and dates of birth and death of the person buried there. Some tombstones, however, may give only the date of death and the person's age at the time of death. If you know the age at death, then calculate the year of birth and record it.

Verses or epitaphs on tombstones may tell a lot about your ancestors.

For example, an epitaph in a Boston cemetery tells how a man took part in America's fight for independence:

Here Rests
Robert Newman
Born in Boston, Mch. 20, 1752

Died in Boston, May 26, 1804
The Patriot who Hung the Signal
Lanterns in the Church Tower,
April 18, 1775

Don't be surprised if you find family members buried in a neglected and forgotten cemetery. One 14-year-old was working on his family history for his Boy Scout Eagle Rank Project. He found his mother's ancestors buried in the country near Franklin, Illinois, their graves half hidden by grasses and shrubs. Only his grandmother, who had attended the last burial there in 1906, remembered where the cemetery was.

The boy also discovered an iron fence surrounding four tombstones engraved with the name "Seymore." All the gravestones outside the fence, however, were inscribed "Seymour." His grandmother explained the mystery. The four people buried inside the fence had a fight with the rest of the family, and so they changed the spelling of their last name. They also had instructed that a fence be built around their graves, so that they wouldn't be with the rest of the family. No one in the family today remembers what the fight was about.

In your search, you may see some words or abbreviations on tombstones that you do not know. Here is a list of common terms:

AE—An abbreviation for *aetatis*, or years of life

B. of L.F. and E.—Brotherhood of Locomotive Firemen and Engineers

B.P.O.E.—Benevolent Protective Order of Elks

D.S.P. or *obit sine prole*—Latin for "died without issue" (children)

D.V.P. or *decessit vita patris*—Latin for "died in father's lifetime"

D.Y.—Died young

G.A.R.—Grand Army of the Republic, or Union Army

H.S. or *hic situs*—Latin for "here is buried"

IHS—The first three letters in *Ihsous*, the Greek word for Jesus

I.O.O.F.—Independent Order of Odd Fellows

O.E.S.—Order of the Eastern Star, an organization for women

V.F.W.—Veterans of Foreign Wars

While you're at the grave site, take pictures or draw sketches in your notebook of the tombstone and any designs on it. Designs, and the shape and size of the stone, are part of the message your ancestor left behind. They may have a special meaning to your ancestor, or they may have been chosen by loved ones to tell what that person did in his or her life. They also may have religious meaning.

For example, brass seals or plates on the stone usually indicate that the person fought in a war or belonged to a certain organization. Broken pillars, often found on a child's tombstone, suggest that a life had been cut short.

Large monuments, such as a tomb, may be in keeping with the personality of the ancestor or with his or her importance to the community and its people. Such monuments usually have been erected by the deceased's family, friends and admirers.

Before you leave your ancestor's grave, check the graves closest to it. Perhaps you'll find an extra relative you didn't know about.

Writing Your Own Epitaph

Here is your chance to decide what message to leave to

your descendants. Many people, especially in the 1800s, wrote their own epitaphs before they died. Some people do it today.

Here are some epitaphs written by pupils in a fourth-grade class in Springfield, Illinois:

Here Lies Kim,
Tall and Slim.
Had hair of gold,
But then grew old.
Her hair turned gray,
And she passed away.

Josh Jacobson was
a very good artist. His drawings
were laughed at when he was alive,
But now we treasure his
drawings. He died of old age at 105.
May He Rest In Peace.

She loved gymnastics, she flipped and flopped.
Until one day she suddenly stopped. Because Sept. 27 was the day of her death and on that day she took her last breath.
The medal above we placed on the grave because she worked so hard,
but never made it to the Olympics.

Taking Information From Records

When you find the record or the tombstone that gives information about your mystery ancestor, make a photocopy of the record, if possible; or take a photograph of the tombstone.

Decide whether the information is what you really wanted,

Your Name
Tells a Story

Why did your parents give you a particular name? Most
people have three names, but you may have more names
appearing on your birth certificate. Your last name, or
surname, is probably the same as your father's. Or, your
last name might be your mother's maiden name and your
father's last name joined with a hyphen.

The surnames on your ancestor chart contain information about your distant ancestors—people who are related to you and lived perhaps 1,000 years ago. Their
surnames may represent their nationalities, their jobs, their
appearances, the places where they lived, or even special
talents. If your last name is Forester, for example, you
might have a distant ancestor who was a wood cutter or
lumberjack.

If your last name is Atwood or De Bussy, you might

have a distant ancestor who was a noble. English nobles often added "atte," meaning "at the," to their surnames. Atwood is from atte Wood. French nobles sometimes added "de," "de la," or "del," meaning "of" or "of the," to their last names.

About 2,500 years ago in Greece, people had only one name, such as Plato or Aristotle. Last names weren't necessary because most communities were so small that everyone knew everyone else. There was no need to ask, "Plato who?"

As communities grew larger, however, it was harder to tell one person from another. So, people added a description after a first name to show the differences among the many Peters or Sarahs in a settlement. Thus, Peter the fish seller in Germany became Peter Fischman, or Peter the fish seller in England became Peter Fisher or Fishman.

But it wasn't until about 1,000 years ago in Italy that people began adopting surnames, which they gave to their children. This custom was soon followed by the Irish, French, English, and then the Germans and other Europeans.

Now let's look at your last name. Which one of these groups does it fit into?

1. Your ancestor may have selected a name that described the place where he lived. For example, Winthrop means "a friendly village." Bradford means "a broad ford," or a place to cross a river. The Japanese name Yamashita means "one who lives below a mountain."

2. Perhaps your ancestor added letters meaning "son of" in his language to the name of his father. In English, for example, John's son became Johnson. In Hebrew, David's son became Ben-David. Or your ancestor may have added a prefix or suffix to his surname to identify himself with his father. Thus, Reilly's son became O'Reilly in Irish and Neill's son became MacNeil in Scottish.

3. Your ancestor may have had a nickname that described a physical feature, reputation, or special talent. For example, John, the strong, became John Strong; and James, the humble person, became James Meek in English or James De Muth in Flemish.

4. Maybe your ancestor was named after a particular season of the year, or an event that happened on his birthday. For example, the surname might be Summer, Winter, Noel, or Holliday, meaning "one born on a holy day."

5. Many people were named after their occupations. Miller, Baker, Parker (park keeper), Cooper (a maker of tubs or casks), Cook (one who bakes pies for sale), and LeFever (French for "blacksmith") are all examples of this type.

There are reference books in your public library that will help you discover what your surname means. They include the following:

New Dictionary of American Family Names by Elston C. Smith. Published by Harper and Row, New York, 1973.

Family Names (How Our Surnames Came to America) by J. N. Hook. Published by Macmillan Publishing Company, New York, 1982.

Dictionary of English and Welsh Surnames by Charles Wareing Bardsley. Published by Genealogical Publishing Company, Baltimore, 1967.

A Handbook of African Names by Ihechukwu Madubuike. Published by Three Continents Press, Washington, D.C., 1976.

You may discover that when your ancestors came to the United States, they changed their names. A German immigrant named Sassamanhausen, for example, changed his name to Sausaman. When black slaves in the United States became free in 1865, they often adopted surnames held by white people. Thus, Jones, Scott, Johnson, Smith, and Brown became common names for blacks. Some blacks named themselves in honor of great Americans, such as Washington and Jefferson.

Now let's look at your first name. Were you named for someone? Do you have the same first name as someone on your ancestor chart? Did one of your ancestral families use the same name over and over again? In earlier times, when many children died in childhood, the same name was often given to more than one child of the same sex to make sure that at least one child with that name would survive.

Students in a class in Durham, North Carolina, recently asked their parents why they had been given that particular first name. Here's what they discovered:

- Black families often gave their children African names. For example, the name Sele is a West African name that means elephant, and Kirabo is an East African name meaning gift.
- Chinese parents may name their children around a single theme. For example, one child might be named Pure Jade, another Shiny Jade.
- Jewish families often give their children Biblical names, such as Daniel, David, and Esther. Some Jewish families name their children after deceased family members so that their dead can be honored.
- American Indians often use names that have to do with nature, such as Black Snake, Honeybee and White Rose.
- Italian and Spanish first names may come from Catholic saints. For example, Anthony comes from Saint Anthony, and Mary and Marie from Jesus' mother.
- Some English names come from locations, such as Craig, meaning "near the crag." A crag is a steep rugged cliff.

The class also discovered that their first names have definite meanings and come from many different languages. Tani is Japanese for "valley," Heather is English for "flowering heath," John is Hebrew for "God is gracious," and Steven is Greek for "crown."

Sometimes a first name tells what language a person's ancestors spoke. For example, a boy named Erik had Scandinavian grandparents. Erik is the Scandinavian word for "knight." Another boy had African ancestors. His name, Agu, is an African name for lion.

A reference book in your public library that will help you discover the meaning and language of your first name is *The Facts on File Dictionary of First Names* by Leslie Dunkling and William Gosling. It is published by Facts on File Publications, New York, 1983.

Why were you given a particular name? What does it mean? What does your surname mean? What do the other surnames on your ancestor chart mean? These are interesting facts to add to your history/mystery notebook.

Sharing Your
Family History

When you've completed your ancestor chart as best you can, you may want to share it with others. Many young people have placed copies of their ancestor charts in local and state libraries and genealogical societies in their areas. The Genealogical Society in Salt Lake City collects family histories. Send them a copy of your ancestor chart and family group sheets, along with a letter to explain that you're donating your work to the society's collection. Be sure to include your name, address, and age. You'll find the address of the society in Chapter 5.

Young people also have written stories about their ancestors and have had them published in state historical magazines. A good example is "In Search of My Grandmother: Ella Nora Critz," included at the end of this chapter. The story was written by a high school senior whose fascination with her deceased grandmother led her to re-search her life and to write a story about her. The story was published in *Texas Historian*, a magazine on Texas history subjects written by young Texan historians and published by the Texas State Historical Association in Austin.

Here are some other ways in which you can share your family history:

- *Calendar:* Make a calendar for your family, marking birthdays, anniversaries, deaths, holidays, yearly activities, and any other important family events that you discovered while researching your family history. You can photocopy the pages and give them as gifts to family members.
- *Newspaper:* Create a family history newspaper. Your feature article could be an interesting story that you discovered about an ancestor while researching your family history. You might include your ancestor chart, favorite family recipes, a gossip column, an interview with a favorite relative, and lost-and-found notices that tell about facts you discovered about ancestors and facts you couldn't find.
- *Family Reunions:* These get-togethers are great opportunities to share your family history, and also to discover more family stories. When you go to the reunion, look for ways in which you might resemble each branch of your family. You might discover that your eyes are from your mother's side of the family, but that your interests are more like those of your relatives on your father's side. Once you start asking questions, who knows where your reunion might lead?

At a family reunion in Peru, Indiana, relatives of Mabel Sausaman learned that Mabel's auburn hair was the same color as her great-grandmother's, Frances Slocum. Mabel had played the part of her great-grandmother in a festival to celebrate Indiana's bicentennial. At the festival, she told how Frances was kidnapped by Indians in Wilkes-Barre, Pennsylvania, when she was four. The family searched for Frances for 50 years before finding her in Indiana. But Frances didn't believe the people were her family until a brother showed her a scar on his finger where it almost had been cut off by an axe. Then she remembered the accident and realized the truth.

It does not matter how you share your family history, but be sure you do share it. Gathering up information about your family, preserving it, and making it available to other family members is important. It is important not only because you find out more about who you are while doing your project, but because today's records no longer provide good information about families. The 1980 federal census, for example, asked detailed information only from families living in every tenth household. Everyone else— perhaps your family included—received short forms to complete.

Thus, the family history you have created is probably the best record on your family in existence. You can be proud of the fact that you've recorded and preserved it. It's a history that people living hundreds of years from now will be excited to read.

In Search of My Grandmother: Ella Nora Critz

by Bergan Critz Norris, Stephen F. Austin High School,

Austin, Texas

(Excerpted from *Texas Historian*, September 1986)

I never knew my maternal grandmother, yet I have been learning about her all my life. My grandmother, Ella Nora "Sugar" Critz Pickle, died of cancer in 1952 when my mother was six, but she left behind admirers who still tell stories about her.

I am fascinated with her, and this fascination inspired me to write this paper. But this is more than just a paper—it is a tribute to Sugar. Sugar attended Austin High School from 1932–35. Fifty years later I, too, am attending Austin High. My mother, Peggy Pickle, graduated from Austin High in 1964. The spring of 1985 marked the fiftieth anniversary of Sugar's graduation from Austin High, and I am now the same age as she was then.

Researching this paper has helped me know the grandmother I never met. I have researched Sugar's school activities, her grades, her social life, her family, and the friends that influenced her as a teenager. My information came from oral interviews with her high school buddies, with members of her family, and with her neighbors while she was growing up. I also researched three years of the *Comet,* the Austin High School yearbook. A scrapbook she kept during her junior and senior years also provided valuable information. Sugar saved everything: newspaper clippings, programs, pictures, dried corsages, wedding announcements, invitations, letters, and poems written by boyfriends—even her first parking ticket. . . .

Sugar was born in 1917 in Georgetown, Texas. Although she was christened Ella Nora, she was called Sugar from infancy. Her mother was Nora Lamb and her father, Richard Critz, was a Williamson County Judge. Sugar had two older brothers, James and Chauncey, and an older sister, Genevieve. Only Chauncey was living at home during Sugar's high school years. . . .

In 1927, the Critzes moved to Austin after Governor Dan Moody appointed Judge Critz to the Commission of Appeals of the Supreme Court of Texas. . . . In 1935, the year Sugar graduated from Austin High, Judge Critz was appointed an Associate Justice of the Texas Supreme Court. . . .

Sugar had grey eyes, and her bobbed hair, which was the look of the 1930s, was parted on the side. Her clothes were padded. . . . Her skirts were cut straight and long. . . . Informal pictures of Sugar have her with arms wrapped around one of her girlfriends and a smile of prankish self-confidence. In formal pictures she smiles demurely. . . .

Sugar belonged to many of the clubs and organizations popular at Austin High. . . .

Literary Societies at Austin High were invitation-only social clubs for girls. In fact, the societies were misnamed because "about the only thing the girls read was their dance cards." The societies were sponsored by an English teacher and met for an hour each week. Semester dues were $5.00 per person which went towards funding a silver tea and a Christmas dance. The silver tea was a day-dance to which the girls brought dates. To these dances, as to all coed functions at Austin High in the 1930s, "If a girl didn't have a date, she didn't go," said Arline Bolm Fitzpatrick, Austin High class of 1936. "Even girls who had a 'steady' expected to be cut in on," said Arline. "It was an embarrassment to dance with the same guy for more than ten seconds!" Because literary societies were so selective, the Texas Legislature outlawed them in 1943 for being discriminatory and "educationally counterproductive.". . .

Sugar also participated in the Boot and Saddle Club, a riding club which met at the Hobby Horse stables near Westenfield Park . . . The horses at the stables could be rented for 50¢ an hour. Today, the trail is a residential street aptly named Bridle Path. . . .

The classes Sugar took are similar to those my mother took in high school and are similar to the classes I am now taking. . . .

Outside of school, Sugar and her friends kept busy swimming at Barton Springs, having slumber parties, double dating, and just "cruising around" in cars. During the summer, because it was so hot and there was no air conditioning, students would swim at Barton Springs for a dime admission charge. They could also eat 10¢ hamburgers and lie on the big rocks across from the bath house. . . .

Double dating was very popular. . . . On dates, students often went to picture shows for 25¢ where they usually sat in the balcony. After the movie, kids went to hamburger joints. . . . Curfews were usually 11:00, or if a couple went to a dance, the girls were expected home immediately after the dance. . . .

One of Sugar's pet peeves was messiness. Like her mother, she was neat and organized. Arline Bolm Fitzpatrick remembers something Sugar told her almost fifty years ago: "You can always tell what kind of house a person has by the front door they keep." This curse of being tidy has been passed on to my mother and to me. . . .

Sugar blackmailed Chauncey into teaching her to drive. When she found out that their parents would disapprove of several things Chauncey had done, she threatened to tell their parents unless Chauncey would teach her to drive his

1933 Buick. So he did. "She'd make your hair stand on top of your head," recalls Chauncey, "because she had a tendency to turn around while driving and talk to those in the back seat. She had trouble parking, too. . . ."

Sugar was mischievous. John Barclay, a neighbor who was a few years older than Sugar, remembers her as being "full of fire and life." He recalls one time when he came home from a date wearing a new Panama suit. Sugar was hiding behind a tree and started squirting him with a garden hose, getting his new suit wet. . . .

Sugar experienced many of the same things my mother and I have experienced. It was eerie looking through her scrapbook of collected memories. I could see Sugar sitting on her bed and pasting her cards, letters, corsages, and articles into place. I wonder if she toyed with the idea of someone finding the scrapbook someday and looking through it with fascination, as my mother and I have done. The yellowed pages which contain Sugar's mementos are a link between us. . . .

EPILOGUE

After Austin High, Sugar attended and later graduated from the University of Texas. In college, she met James Jarrell "Jake" Pickle of Big Spring. They married in 1942. Their daughter, Peggy, my mother, was born in 1946 and graduated from Austin High in 1964. In 1960, eight years after Sugar's death, Jake married Beryl Bolton McCarroll. She is the grandma I've grown up with. In 1963, Jake Pickle was elected U.S. Representative from Texas' 10th Congressional District. . . .

Here's another family history, written for a school project.

My Most Interesting Ancestor

by Brian Lee, Brea Junior High School, Brea, California

Brian's story is based on an interview with his father, who told of Yung Chang Lee from memory. Brian's family adopted western names in China because they belonged to a Christian church.

My grandfather, Yung Chang Lee, was born on February 5, 1900, in Szechuan, China. When he was eleven, the Ching Dynasty ended, and the Republic of China began. He went to Shanghai for a college education when he was eighteen. At twenty years of age, he joined the military academy and graduated in one year because the government needed soldiers to fight the rebels who were trying to gain control of China. In 1928, the rebels were defeated so he went back to Szechuan and married Ju-Tien Wang.

When Japan invaded China in 1937, he led the troops against the enemy to defend his homeland. On August 16, 1938, his eldest son, Francis, was born, and on April 29, 1940, my father, Steven, was also born. Since they were a military family, they moved to wherever he was stationed. On September 6, 1944, his first daughter, Stella, was born.

When World War II ended, the family moved back to Szechuan, and my grandfather was promoted to a one-star general. That same year, communists started fighting against the government of China. He was back in the war. Unfortunately, he was shot in the leg and captured by the communists. [He was held prisoner] for three years. In 1949, he was released and sent back to Szechuan. Within a few months, the whole family was forced to flee to Taipei, Taiwan, because they were a military family and communists had surrounded the city. In December of 1949, they had to start over in Taipei because, in their hurried rush from Szechuan, they had to leave almost everything behind.

For a while, the family had to raise chickens and sell eggs and vegetables. On September 26, 1950, the youngest daughter, Joyce, was born. From 1951 to 1961, my grandfather delivered newspapers, in order to support the family. In 1961, he got a job working for the local government. But, in 1964, tragedy struck. He had a heart attack and was paralyzed for six months. He recovered only enough to walk with a cane.

In August of 1965, his second son, Steve, went to the United States. In 1970, my grandfather went to an old-age home in Taipei to live out the rest of his life. On March 4, 1973, he passed away peacefully.

Directory

This directory gives you more places to look for information about your ancestors. The information can lead you to many different sources to help you complete your ancestor chart and family group sheets.

IF YOU NEED:

HERE'S WHAT YOU DO:

An address of a genealogical society

Look in the public library for the *Directory of Historical Societies and Agencies in the United States and Canada*, Tracey Linton Craig, editor and compiler. It is published by the American Association for State and Local History, Nashville, Tennessee.

Information about what records are available in the county courthouse, and whom to contact for records or copies in each state and county

Look in your public library for *The Handy Book for Genealogists*, George B. Everton Sr., editor. It is published by Everton Publishers, Inc., Logan, Utah.

An address of a state office handling the registration of vital records, such as records of birth and death

Look in the reference section in your public library for a copy of "Where to Write for Vital Records: Births, Deaths, Marriages and Divorces." Or, you can purchase a copy by writing the U. S. Department of Health and Human Services, U. S. Government Printing Office, Washington, D.C. 20402.

Military record of an ancestor in World War I, World War II, Korean War, or Vietnam War

Write to the National Military Personnel Records Center, 9700 Page Blvd., St. Louis, Missouri 63132. Only the soldier may obtain these records, or a member of the soldier's family if that person can prove that the soldier is deceased. For more information, see the section about writing federal agencies in Chapter 5.

Military record of an ancestor in a war before World War I (all military records will give you the color of your ancestor's eyes)

Write to the National Archives, Central Reference Division, General Services Administration, Washington, D.C. 20408. Your letter will be routed to the correct office.

Naturalization record (an immigrant's oath of allegiance to the United States)

If the record isn't in the National Archives or one of its regional branches, check the county courthouse where the naturalization took place.

Passenger arrival record (lists passengers who arrived at ports on the Atlantic Ocean, Gulf of Mexico, and a few inland ports; most of the lists are for the years 1820 to 1945)

Write to the National Archives.

Index